DRILLING AND FRACKING

GLOBAL CITIZENS: ENVIRONMENTALISM

Published in the United States of America by Cherry Lake Publishing
Ann Arbor, Michigan
www.cherrylakepublishing.com

Content Adviser: Michael Rockett MS, Natural resources

Reading Adviser: Marla Conn MS, Ed., Literacy specialist, Read-Ability, Inc.

Photo Credits: © Calin Tatu/Shutterstock.com, cover, 1; © Merlin74/Shutterstock.com, 5; © Mikhail Starodubov/Shutterstock
.com, 6; © Lonny Garris/Shutterstock.com, 8; © Polina Petrenko/Shutterstock.com, 10; © Samjaw/Shutterstock.com, 13;
© Nate Allred/Shutterstock.com, 14; © SDubi/Shutterstock.com, 16; © kimson/Shutterstock.com, 19; © Paul D Smith/
Shutterstock.com, 20; © Monkey Business Images/Shutterstock.com, 22, 28; © Lisa S./Shutterstock.com, 25; © didesign021/
Shutterstock.com, 26

Library of Congress Cataloging-in-Publication Data
Names: Labrecque, Ellen, author.
Title: Drilling and fracking / Ellen Labrecque.
Description: Ann Arbor : Cherry Lake Publishing, 2017. | Series: Global citizens. Environmentalism |
    Audience: Grades 4 to 6. | Includes bibliographical references and index.
Identifiers: LCCN 2016058617| ISBN 9781634728683 (hardcover) | ISBN 9781634729574 (pdf) |
    ISBN 9781534100466 (pbk.) | ISBN 9781534101357 (hosted ebook)
Subjects: LCSH: Petroleum industry—Environmental aspects. | Fossil fuels—Environmental aspects—
    Juvenile literature. | Petroleum engineering—Juvenile literature.
Classification: LCC TD195.P4 L33 2017 | DDC 333.8/230973—dc23
LC record available at https://lccn.loc.gov/2016058617

Cherry Lake Publishing would like to acknowledge the work of the Partnership for 21st Century Learning.
Please visit *www.p21.org* for more information.

Printed in the United States of America
Corporate Graphics

ABOUT THE AUTHOR

Ellen Labrecque has written over 100 books for children. She is passionate about being a friend to the environment and taking care of our planet. She lives in Pennsylvania with her husband, Jeff, and her two young "editors," Sam and Juliet. She loves running, hiking, and reading.

TABLE OF CONTENTS

CHAPTER 1

History: Fossil Fuels

Environmentalism is a big word. But its meaning is simple. Practicing environmentalism means being a friend of Earth and all its creatures. Environmentalists want to keep our air healthy, our land clean, and our water fresh. They want to take care of our plants and animals by making sure our planet remains a safe place to live. Some environmentalists focus on encouraging people to stop polluting. Others encourage people to **recycle**. One of the most important environmental jobs is to teach people the dangerous costs of drilling and fracking for oil and natural gas.

The Story of Fossil Fuels

Earth has been around for 4.5 billion years. About 350 million years ago, tiny **organisms** died and sank to the bottom of

Fossil fuels were formed during the Paleozoic Era.

swamps around the world. Over the next millions of years, these organisms **decomposed** and transformed into **petroleum**. The petroleum's location determined its form: gas (natural gas) or liquid (oil). The natural gas formed in deeper and hotter locations than the oil. The gas and oil underneath Earth are called **fossil fuels**. Today, we use fossil fuels to run almost all our energy sources. We use them to run our cars, trains, airplanes, and even ships. We also use them to cook and to heat and light our houses and buildings.

People have been drilling for oil as far back as the year 347.

The average commercial plane needs at least 1 gallon (4 liters) of fuel every second.

In China, they used tools made from bamboo to dig down as deep as 800 feet (244 meters). They dug where oil was discovered seeping up to the surface. Back then, oil was used to make tools and weapons and to light torches.

In 1859, American businessman George Bissell drilled for oil in Titusville, Pennsylvania. He discovered oil after drilling down only 70 feet (21 meters). This was the first oil well in the United States. Bissell's discovery started the oil boom across the entire world. Twenty-six years later, the first automobile was invented and ran on gasoline. Then, in 1903, Henry Ford began producing cars on a large scale, selling millions to the American public. The more people bought cars, the more they needed gasoline. The demand for gasoline made from oil skyrocketed. Drillers began calling it "black gold."

Fracking, or hydraulic fracturing, has only been around since the 1940s. Fracking is when a tube filled with chemicals is injected at a high pressure into a rock formation 8,000 feet (2.4 kilometers) below Earth's surface. This pressure opens up fissures, or cracks, in the rocks that allow natural gas to seep out through a pipe. The pipe brings the gas to the surface.

This is a fracking rig in Colorado.

Fracking began on a large scale in the 1990s when scientists invented tools that could drill not only vertically (up and down) but also horizontally (side to side). This allowed workers to get to gas in places that they didn't think was possible. They could now drill thousands of feet in any direction and obtain more gas.

Dangers of Fracking and Oil Drilling

Even though much of the world's population depends on oil and gas in their everyday lives, fracking and oil drilling can do permanent damage to Earth. Sometimes forests have to be cut down to make room for fracking or oil drilling. This affects the wildlife living in those forests. In addition, fracking threatens our clean water supplies. Devastating oil spills can ruin land and water sources.

Fossil fuels are **nonrenewable resources**. This means that someday they will run out. If we keep using oil and gas at our current pace, they could run out by 2071. Something that formed millions of years ago could be completely gone after less than 200 years of overuse.

Once oil and gas are extracted, they need to be **refined**. The process of refining fossil fuels contributes to **climate change**.

Parts of forests are cleared away to drill for oil.

Climate change is believed to be melting polar glaciers, causing sea levels to rise, and creating extreme and dangerous weather throughout the world. It is causing **droughts** in some places and **monsoons** in other places. As a result, more animals all over the globe, on land, under the sea, and in the air, may be threatened with **extinction**.

Developing Questions

Environmentalists believe we rely too much on fossil fuels. Reread this passage again. Why do you think environmentalists believe this? What are ways we can cut back on the use of fossil fuels?

A close-ended question is a question that can be answered with a simple yes or no. An open-ended question is one that needs more thought when answering. The questions above are meant to be open-ended questions. They are meant to make you think about ways you can help cut back on fossil fuels rather than just answering yes or no.

CHAPTER 2

Geography: Oil Drilling and Fracking All Over the World

Scientists know how to find and dig for oil and gas better than ever. We have developed the most advanced tools that now make hard-to-reach fossil fuels reachable. About 100 countries around the world produce oil, and about 95 countries produce natural gas. But the more we refine or burn fossil fuels, the more we risk contributing to climate change. Digging for oil can also destroy forests and leave animals without homes. Much of the Amazon rainforest in South America is being destroyed to dig for oil and gas.

Drilling and Spilling

More than 1 million tons of oil are accidentally spilled every

A fishing boat accidentally leaks oil into the ocean.

Many birds died during the Gulf of Mexico oil well explosion.

year. Oil spills are incredibly harmful to birds and many forms of marine life. One of the worst spills that has ever happened was from a 2010 explosion of an oil well in the Gulf of Mexico. The well gushed about 2.5 million gallons (9.5 million L) of oil each day for 85 days until the well was finally fixed. Eleven workers died in the explosion, and the oil leak killed thousands of birds and other marine life. Many of the surviving birds, turtles, and mammals were covered in oil. An estimated 1,100 miles (1,770 km) of the Gulf Coast shoreline is now polluted.

The Danger to Water

Fracking can also ruin water supplies. In order to frack, a lot of different chemicals have to be used. These chemicals can seep into water supplies. People who live near fracking sites all over the United States have gotten sick from drinking contaminated water and breathing in contaminated air. The people living near these sites have much higher rates of breathing problems, cancer, and skin conditions than people who don't live near the sites. According to current US laws, companies that run a fracking business don't need to reveal what chemicals are being used for fracking. This means that when chemicals do end up in

Some scientists believe that the rise in earthquakes is linked to fracking.

people's water supplies, the fracking companies aren't held responsible.

Earthquakes

Fracking can cause earthquakes. The waste fluid left over from fracking is disposed of into special wells deep underground. This fluid can seep into faults, which can cause a quake. Until 2008, Oklahoma averaged just one or two moderate earthquakes a year. Since then, the state began fracking on a large scale, and the average number is now more than 100 a year. Many countries around the world have banned fracking, including France, Bulgaria, Germany, and Scotland. Vermont and New York are the only states in the United States that have outlawed this practice.

Gathering and Evaluating Sources

Different types of maps show different things to people. A political map shows the borders of countries and states. Physical maps show landscape features, such as mountains and rivers. Some environmentalists use Threat Maps. These maps allow people to see if they live near a place that has harmful air pollution from oil drilling and fracking sites. Check out these maps at www.oilandgasthreatmap.com/threat-map/national-map.

CHAPTER 3

Civics: Can Anything Be Done?

In order to stop climate change from getting worse, scientists think the world needs to cut back on drilling and fracking. This is not easy, though. People need all this oil and gas for fuel when they drive cars and trucks. Buses, trains, ships, and airplanes need fossil fuels to run, too. We also use oil and gas to heat our homes, schools, and stores. Although our supplies won't last forever, there are trillions of dollars' worth of fossil fuels still in the ground. And we have more technologies that allow us to dig than we ever had before. This means we are doing more digging, not less. We shouldn't be relying on fossil fuels alone.

This is a wind turbine plant between Denmark and Sweden.

Different Kinds of Energy

We need to use more **renewable resources** to get our energy. One form of renewable energy is wind power. Power from the wind can be turned into energy to power our electricity and heat our homes. **Wind turbines** do the job of capturing the wind without polluting the air. Denmark leads the world in wind power use. Thirty percent of the country's electricity is powered by wind.

There are still challenges with wind energy, however. Scientists haven't figured out a way to store the energy from wind in large

The world's largest electric car charging station opened in Norway in 2016.

amounts. It is also expensive to build, install, and operate these turbines. But work is being done to fix these problems. Scientists hope that by 2020, 10 percent of the world's electricity will be wind powered.

Another way we can use renewable energy is by driving electric cars. Electric cars run on rechargeable batteries instead of gasoline. The country of Norway is leading the electric car charge. Twenty-four percent of the cars there are now electric. One way that Norway is able to encourage people to use electric cars is by setting up charging stations all over the country. Instead of stopping at a gas station to fill up, people stop and charge up.

Developing Claims and Using Evidence

Pretend somebody says, "Burning fossil fuels does not harm Earth." Can you find evidence against this statement? Can you find evidence supporting it? Using the evidence you find, form your own opinion. Do you think oil companies will report that digging for oil is bad for the environment? Why or why not?

Educators believe in teaching kids about the environment.

Other types of natural, renewable energy sources are solar (getting energy from the sun), hydropower (getting energy from water), and geothermal (getting energy from below Earth's surface). These types of energy are used all over the world, but much more can still be done.

Educate

The more people understand the consequences of drilling and fracking, the better off Earth will be. The National Center for Science Education is an organization that supports teachers across the country who teach about climate change and the dangers of burning fossil fuels. Some people say that burning fossil fuels isn't hurting Earth. Others think that we are powerless to change. Teachers need to educate our children now, so they grow up knowing the facts and dangers, as well as the possible solutions. To learn about the National Center for Science Education and how your school can get involved, visit www.ncse.com/climate.

Top Five Oil-Producing Countries

1. Russia
2. Saudi Arabia
3. United States
4. Iraq
5. China

CHAPTER 4

Economics: The Cost of Fracking and Drilling

When oil and gas become plentiful, their prices go down. The more drilling and fracking done, the cheaper oil and gas prices are. When prices are low, people use more fossil fuels. This means oil and gas companies keep digging to find more. This excessive digging comes at a price; it affects our environment and our health. How can we stop this cycle?

Carbon Tax

One way to slow down all this drilling is by creating a carbon tax. A carbon tax is a charge by the government to individuals, companies, and businesses based on how much fossil fuel they burn. The more fossil fuels a person or company burns, the more

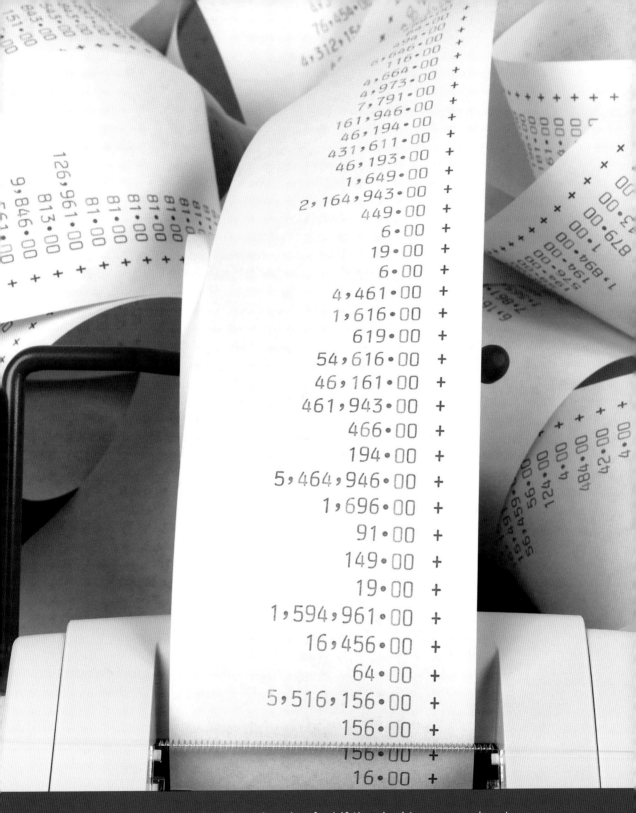

People may think twice about burning fuel if they had to pay a carbon tax.

San Francisco residents using solar panels can receive up to $10,000 from the government depending on their income.

they are charged. This type of tax would hopefully change people's behavior and encourage them to burn less fossil fuels and use other forms of energy.

Go Green for Money

Governments around the world pay companies and individuals to switch to renewable energy. The United States offers tax incentives to companies and individuals that use **solar panels** for heat and energy. The government of Costa Rica is building a high-speed electric rail across its country that will be completed by 2020. The hope is that people will stop using their

Communicating Conclusions

Before reading this book, did you know about the dangers of fracking and oil drilling? Now that you know more, why do you think this is an important issue? Share your knowledge about fracking and drilling and the importance of stopping more of this from happening. Every week, look up different organizations that work to stop fracking and drilling. Share what you learn with friends at school or with family at home.

There are many industries that contribute to clean energy discoveries, including 3D printing.

cars and use the high-speed electric train instead. The air pollution in India has become so bad that it accounts for almost 500,000 deaths a year. To help combat the air pollution, India's government has invested millions of dollars into building more electric cars. The government has also doubled the taxes on fossil fuels being produced in or imported into the country. The money from these taxes goes to the National Clean Energy Fund, which is used to create more clean energy projects.

Clean Energy Jobs

Creating clean energy also means creating new clean energy jobs. China is leading the way, with more than 3.4 million people working in the entire renewable energy industry. Germany leads Europe with 370,000 of its people working to stop climate change. The United States is leading the world in solar energy jobs, with close to 200,000 people working in this industry.

Taking Informed Action

Do you want to help limit oil drilling and fracking? There are many ways you can get involved and many different organizations you can explore. Check them out online. Here are three to start your search:

- *Environment America—Stop Fracking Our Future: Discover ways you can help stop fracking in your state.*
- *Food & Water Watch—Fracking: Learn more about the harmful effects of fracking.*
- *The Nature Conservancy Carbon Calculator: Calculate your own **carbon footprint**!*

Think About It

There are more than 7 billion people living on Earth. It is estimated that by 2050, 9.7 billion people will live here. Population growth and burning fossil fuels are linked together. The more people on our planet, the more people will need fossil fuels to heat their homes and drive their cars. Scientists think all these new people need to understand what drilling and burning fossil fuels do to our planet. Providing education about the hazards of fracking and drilling is the first step to a cleaner future. How might learning about these hazards help people and companies switch to alternative energy sources? Why might it be difficult for them to switch from fossil fuels to renewable energy? Use the data you find in your research to support your argument.

For More Information

FURTHER READING

Bang, Molly, and Penny Chisholm. *Buried Sunlight: How Fossil Fuels Have Changed the Earth.* New York: Scholastic, 2014.

Fridell, Ron. *Earth-Friendly Energy.* Minneapolis: Lerner Publishing, 2009.

Spilsbury, Richard, and Louise Spilsbury. *Let's Discuss Energy Resources: Fossil Fuel Power.* New York: The Rosen Publishing Group, 2012.

WEB SITES

NASA—Climate Kids: Carbon's Travels
http://climatekids.nasa.gov/menu/carbons-travels
Learn about the history of fossil fuels from experts at the National Aeronautics and Space Administration (NASA).

National Geographic—Climate Connections
http://ngm.nationalgeographic.com/climateconnections
Find all kinds of information about climate change.

The United States Department of Energy
www.energy.gov
Learn all about the energy sources in the United States.

GLOSSARY

carbon footprint (KAHR-buhn FUT-print) a measure of the amount of carbon dioxide produced by a person, object, or organization and released into the atmosphere

climate change (KLYE-mit CHAYNJ) a change in normal weather patterns over a long period of time

decomposed (dee-kuhm-POHZD) rotted or broken down

droughts (DROUTS) periods of dry weather

environmentalism (en-vye-ruhn-MEN-tuhl-iz-uhm) working to protect the air, water, animals, and plants from pollution and other harmful things

extinction (ik-STING-shun) no longer existing or having died out

fossil fuels (FAH-suhl FYOOLZ) oil, coal, and gas formed from the remains of animals and plants that died and decayed millions of years ago

monsoons (mon-SOONZ) seasons marked by heavy rains

nonrenewable resources (non-rih-NOO-uh-buhl REE-sors-iz) things of value from the earth, like fossil fuels, that cannot be replaced and can be eventually used up

organisms (OR-guh-niz-uhmz) living things, such as plants or animals

petroleum (puh-TROH-lee-uhm) a thick, flammable, dark-colored oil found in rocks

recycle (ree-SYE-kuhl) to break something down in order to make something new from it

refined (rih-FINED) to be purified or have unwanted matter removed from a substance such as oil

renewable resources (rih-NOO-uh-buhl REE-sors-iz) natural power, such as wind, that will never be used up and can be used again and again

solar panels (SOH-lur PAN-uhlz) materials that form part of a surface and are used to absorb the sun's rays

wind turbines (WIND TUR-binz) machines that capture energy from the wind, which eventually is converted to electricity

INDEX